a fire like you

Also by Upile Chisala

soft magic
nectar

a fire like you

UPILE CHISALA

Andrews McMeel
PUBLISHING®

For Sakhe.
Your love is the kindest of creatures.

CONTENTS

Wound

-

And if you let it,
fear will gladly tell your story.

As Black as Tax

Here,
We were never once children.

Here, our mothers, like Mary, birthed saviors.
Our only purpose is to redeem.

Month-end is for working miracles, little black
Jesuses.

"Let there be light and water, rent and bread."

Caring Pains

Here,

To be woman is to care hard,
Care until it kills you.

Inheritance #1

I can't decide whether it was borrowed or a thing
of the blood.
Wherever I got it from then,
I am choosing not to claim it now.

Gogo

I guess your heart needed the rest after a whole life of holding everyone in it.

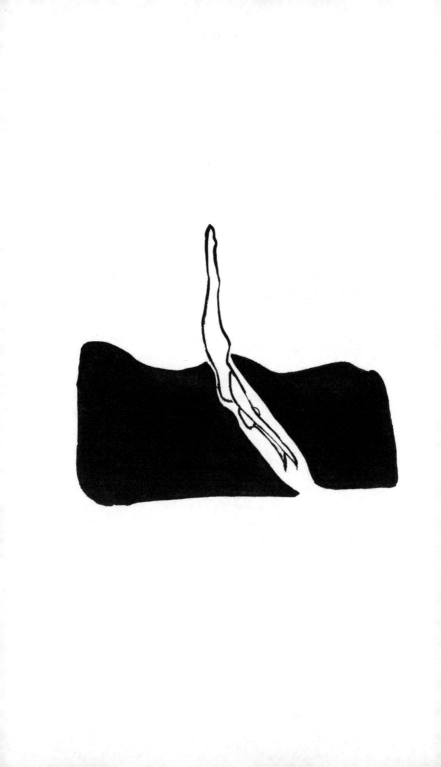

Swim Class

You cannot dive into their
mouths and fish out a "sorry";
it's never worked that way.
And what good is a "sorry" you had to drown for?

You Are Not a Mender of Men

I want to break the messiah in you.
Not everyone is yours to save.

Inheritance #2

Listen,
Someone has to listen to the "Go"
And the "Run"
And the "Don't look back"
And have the stomach to leave like your father,
Even if just this once.

You can be that someone, the someone who
makes joy on new ground.

Sometimes

I walk in, hurt from the day.
How much tired is in black living?

I want light bones and lots of money.
I want it easier.
I want it white with little sorry.

Equal Parts Nothing and Everything

You hurt best,
And I wish you'd stay gone the longest.

It's not the blood or the bone or the good years;
I think I just love you cause I can.
Cause it comes easier than hating you
And hurts less.

"When Will You Go Back?"

What if

"Back" is a story you want to spit out?
"Back" is your grandmother's body in the ground?
"Back" is a heavy heart?
"Back" is always a hungry pocket?
"Back" is where your dreams give up on you?

Familiar

Something as brutal as you,
As fist-like and unaware,
With a cruel history, in the bone
And in the mouth,
With little prospect of peace,
Always on the wrong side,
Something as brutal as you walks in, and I embrace it.

I embrace it knowingly.

It Ended as Sourly as It Did Because

We were two bruised things
Behaving poorly.
Always going wound for wound
And troubled father for troubled father.

Dredging up dirt and trauma.
Nothing was sacred, everything was a weapon,
No one was safe.
This is the damage dance.

Fire still can't be put out with gasoline.
Love and violence have never been friends.

a fire like you

-

Right in the meat of our love I knew it,
I knew it like my palm,
This would be a story filled with bones.

Match

In some homes,
Like ours,
Both the betrayal and the forgiveness
Were ruthless and constant
And undeserved.

Waiting Bodies. Weighty Bodies.

Every time I mean to write about my body, I laugh.
How can someone be so un-in-love with this
luscious, overflowing
Concoction of thigh
And dark, desirable things?
How can that someone be me?
How dare I!

How I look in the mirror and grieve!
How do I wake up in hate?
And will I ever get tired of trying to make small
of my heavy,
To make light of my darkness,
To see beauty where I see ugly?

Someone said they would die for a body like this.

Well, someone is dying to leave this body,
No, someone is dying to love this body again.

A Father Is a Something

Dad,

I won't carry your fate forward.

I'll show up in celebration of everyone who celebrates me.

I will be the one promise you will never break.

Abbreviation

We learned it when we were younger,
There are things you mustn't ask.
There are uncles who go thin,
And stop laughing,
And disappear.
And there are aunts who are left behind to take
the pills,
And stay alive,
And pay the rent,
And never speak ill.

We learned it when we were younger,
Some things hurt and hurt again.

a fire like you

-

1. You didn't break God's heart.

2. We can't always spot the wolves.

3. Even people you love can be beasts.

4. Even beds can be hell.

5. Even our bodies can feel like foreign countries. Countries we never wanted to visit. Countries that are on fire. Countries we want to run from. Countries that will never love us back.

6. You didn't break God's heart.

7. Don't blame yourself for their bite.

8. You didn't know you were walking into a mouth.

9. Even people you love can be beasts.

The Thing About Souls

You are gone in so many ways,
But here in new ones.

You have us by the heart;
We'll always be yours, and you'll always be ours.

Part Prayer, Part Plea

Is being someone's daughter sure punishment?

Will I spend my whole life begging for permission
to breathe?

A Mercy

I want to be as careful with my words as I can.
Because I am the kind to run into my mouth and
say things less lovely than I meant them. Regret it,
regret it in the belly. Here is my offering, ugly and
sharp but true.

It always felt good, but it never felt right. And
endings can be remarkable things if we let them.

What Was Lost

Losing will always feel fresh
And under-grieved.

You were the sister I chose.
And I was your willing disciple.

Somewhere,
A nightclub remembers us dancing.

There, our friendship
Is still breathing.

A Few Things You May Reconsider

1. That knife of a mouth.

2. A liking for the bottle, if it comes with a disliking for yourself.

3. Hiding hot anger under thick laughter.

4. Talking yourself out of joy more times than into it.

Sold Out

"Trust me, you'll regret it," they say.

Trust me,
if my father had even one "sorry" to offer,
I'd buy out the front row and listen.

-

Home for you was always hard.
Someone was always raising their voice,
The other was always wanting out.

So much running under one roof.
So much longing in a single space.

Addendum

All we learned,
we the children they supposedly stayed for,
was that misery was home and right and ours.

Softness Is a Gift in Worlds and Homes as Hard as These Ones

Your mother has kind eyes,
Is sorry she said those things you know she'll say
again tomorrow,
Wishes you weren't so set on being so soft and
breakable,
Wants you to take her abuse with a smile.

Small Violences and Other Lies

Because you say it with the sweetest parts of you,
In the sweetest voice,
Out of the sweetest mouth,
I am honeyed by it.
And fall into it.
And crawl under it.
Suddenly, I am the sorry one
And you are the savior.
And all your cruel things are gone and forgotten.
This is a violence.

You tell me I live in a panic
That my favorite houses are the ones that shake.
That I wouldn't know love if it called me by
my name.
This is how you like to cut me down and call me
twisted.
This is how you forget you are the danger.
This a violence too.

The art of turning someone against themselves.
The art of making someone small.
The art of tearing a pride limb from limb.
The art of having the last word, the word that
matters, the word that holds water.

This is a violence,
and in love there is no small violence
and no rug to
sweep it under.

a fire like you

-

I haven't quite figured out what the loneliness is meant to teach me, especially when it crawls into rooms I've filled with people.

Borders

These lines drawn crooked
draw blood so neatly.

a fire like you

-

I miss you in a very real way
But I'm far too proud
And tired
And angry
To rebuild that bridge.

Martyr/Mother/Magician

Your mother,
like mine,
lives in between mourning and rejoicing.
Took whatever joy offered, however little,
and promised to make love out of it.

But you,
and I,
and even she
can learn the way out of any love that requires
our smallness.

a fire like you

-

You can give and give and come out the other end
tired and longing.

-

You should know,
burning is not the only way to come to poetry.

You don't have to pry open a wound to have a story
worth telling.

-

I have been grieving a lot of things that needed to die in me.

Hunger

Please Note

The very first step is believing you deserve joy.

All That Grew

There is a long list of things I wish this life had or
hadn't given me,
But now that I am here, having lived with and
without,
I know life was only preparing me for myself
and I was worth the wait.

Gently

Darling,

There's so much life in this place,
everything is begging you to breathe.

a fire like you

-

1. Are you ungrateful for wanting your
   forgiveness to look nothing like your mother's?

   No

2. You were taught that men are gods
   That God is a man
   That God is your father
   That your father is God.

3. In your story, "home" and "wound" are synonymous
   Just like "mother" and "worshipper."

4. And what kind of love grows from a wound?

5. Are you ungrateful if you celebrate the day
   you left home,
   I mean wound, I mean mother,
   worshipper, father, and God?

   No

6. Growing up where you did and how you did
   You know good and well
   That staying is only half of the story.

   It may kick you in the pride every time.
   But the work of keeping a love warm and
   living is always worth it.

There Isn't a Fire Around Like You

Because you have it
—Time—
and having it is a blessing,
spend some of it
learning how not to be afraid of yourself.

a fire like you

-

Saying it isn't far from living it
Of course, only
if you believe in that kind of thing
Your mouth or your magic
Your magic or your mouth.

Grace

You've got to make right with your story.
None of this half living and hot anger.
None of this leaving yourself and falling into
people.
None of this staying cause their warmth comes
with little work.
None of this settling for smallness.

You've got to make right with your story,
So you can be a home to yourself.
Because no one can give you as good a life
as you can.

It Will Serve You Most

While you're at it,
Learn accountability.
Learn it well.

Even with kind intentions, you too could be the
beast in a story.

-

Your witchery is knowing you're yours,

when all your training has taught you to be
someone else's.

-

If it is all burning and misery ahead,

I hope the version of myself that is tired of rising
from the ashes in the end

Shows up and keeps me from dancing into the fire
to begin with.

a fire like you

-

You were taught to work miracles for everyone
but yourself.
A messiah to others but barely a friend of your own.
These, darling, are things you must undo before
you become undone.

-

A list of things you've braved lately:

Bills that linger.

Silence that cuts.

Mothers who lug around pain.

Gods who don't show up.

The dead who aren't getting any rest.

Brothers who sink into their father's habits.

Fathers who aren't sorry.

Lovers who make doors out of your tiniest flaws
and walk out with parts of you.

But, darling, remember healing never forgets to
come to soften the day.

These are things you will survive.

a fire like you

-

It will go how it will go;
Either way, I will arm myself with gladness.

Ready

Now that you've chosen peace, prepare for it.
Make yourself a home for the healing.
Half of the work is readying your heart.
So when joy walks in, you know it's yours
and that you deserve it.

a fire like you

-

Darling,

There is no shame in a fresh beginning.

There is no shame in a fresh beginning.

There is no shame in a fresh beginning.

There is no shame in a fresh beginning.

There is no shame in a fresh beginning.

There is no shame in a fresh beginning.

There is no shame in a fresh beginning.

There is no shame in a fresh beginning, only grace and gratitude.

Find a Quiet Place to Practice

Some people don't sit with themselves long
enough to learn to love from the inside out.

a fire like you

-

I hope the thrill of leaving yourself wears off
Soon and completely.
Because when it comes to it, when it comes
Right down to it, you're the one you need.

Once the Water Goes

This life will push you, my darling.
So you'll have to learn
First to cry for crying's sake.
And then get up and push it back.

-

You are working on having the backbone for this life;
every joy you conjure is a blessing,
every part of you that wants another day is golden.

You are worth the care and celebration.

Some Truths Are Just as Persistent Tomorrow

The wine is as makeshift a solution as the lover.
If you want a story that doesn't reek of regret,
you'll have to crawl out of your old ways and learn
to be honest.

-

Darling,

You have to do it with intention
or not do it at all;
practicing joy with only half your heart
is as good as daring darkness.

a fire like you

-

Please have the audacity to love yourself a little harder.

A Love Poem for a Tryer

You're as much magic as you were yesterday,
Even if today is filled with shaking the misery,
Dancing off the tired,
Deeply wanting an out.

You're as much magic as you were yesterday.

a fire like you

I Like My Black Joy Full-Fat and Unrepentent

Given all the tragedy, the harsh parts and addictions,
The room was black and still every bit holy.
A magic was loose here.

We took it,
laughed from the belly,
and decided on full lives.

A Story and Another

You'll meet yourself one day
And it may terrify you to know that there's more
And it's magnificent.

Poetry Won't Suffer if You Smile Now

"Be a dear
Hurt for us here
Forget the wound
Knit the words together
Hurt for us here,

"We'll pay good money
We'll cry those tears
We'll go back to our homes
And forget we left yours shaking," they say.

Honestly,

I can't keep pulling from the ruin. I can't keep
returning to the ruin. I can't keep being the ruin.

You would like my trauma, hot and heavy and at
the snap of your fingers. I know myself to give it,
to pull it from somewhere and pour it where you
please. This is a story you know, but I tell it over

and over, because it's easier to tell than the story
that scares you. The one of joy, the one of how I've
learned to listen to my sadness, to hold room for
it without handing it the house. The one where I
accept only good things and revel in them. I have
spent what feels like a thousand lifetimes living
in hurt and thinking it the only life I was worthy
of. But now, having made it to other side, the side
black girls are often told they'll never find, I know
that this is a vicious lie and real life is waiting for
us to begin it.

The Hunger

Dancing hand in hand with her desire,
She is the love she waited for living.
Someone ought to tell it right and straight,

We were always meant for ourselves.

a fire like you

-

Excuse me while I shake the table
And make myself the proudest.
Maybe I am not always the daughter you clap for
But I am mine for the choosing, and in that is a peace.

Be Still and Know I Am God

Gogo, you told me that was one of your favorite
songs. I'm sorry I'm still not good at being still and
I've never quite got round to knowing God.

But even if I don't cross my legs like you asked,
and I pick fights with Jesus like you asked me not
to, I am still many things you can be glad in. Just
trust and know that I am still many things you can
be glad in.

a fire like you

-

You offer up forgiveness as if it were your name
And in the end
Whose peace are you really keeping?

Remember Kindness

Please remember, if no part of you is yourself,
every part of you suffers.

A Promise to Mama Maya

Maybe I won't learn right away.
And I'll make the same mistake twice.
But this I can promise.
I'll dance each time I rise.

\-

Expect love
and change
and growth
and failure
and goodness
and all the other symptoms of a life lived to its fullest.

a fire like you

-

It might surprise you
That I still walk in love
And count myself blessed

It might surprise you
But it doesn't surprise me
I have always known myself to be a fire.

Living Is Trying and Trying and We Are Beautiful for It

Yes, I've got all kinds of misery;
I've got it and it's got me.
But I've been growing the language to cast it out,
And the feet to dance it gone,
And the bravery to let something kinder take its place.

I can't help but think of myself as some kind of beautiful for bothering.

Swoon

Fruit

Faced with a love like this,
I now know how the thing that craves goodness in
the deepest parts of us wins in the end.

The Sixth Day of December

Love can be sudden but still certain.

You could be folding clothes in the swelter
In a small town known only for its smallness
And look up and see his heart for what it is
And that's enough to say "I love you"
And that's enough to mean it.

-

I come home to you in a hurry
Always a hurry.

I dragged my feet as a child.
It drove everyone mad.
I couldn't drag my feet any slower.

Home wasn't too bad, it was just hard.
Hard enough not to miss it as much.
Hard enough not to hurry to.

a fire like you

-

It is more amazement than doubt.
I'm used to people loving me
or saying they do
or at least acting it.
But you,
more than in love,
are in care with me,
and it's all the right kinds of overwhelming.

Your Coat and Your Heart Too

You say the sweetest things without even trying.
They just slip out of you, easy and free.

You hold all the right words
And wrap them around me, and they fit.

I Think the Furniture Knows

What we make is magic.
We crawl under and over and into each other.
We make the sheets blush.
The walls have never seen an act quite like us.

a fire like you

-

When good love dares to hold you,
and you are caught between accepting the heat of
it all
or running,

choose the fire.

After the Shock

I have enough pride in my heart to feign
indifference.
Be around when you're around, smile but sigh in
my bones.
I am troubled in this way.
But if it broke me once, it could break me again.
And I'd rather not dare it.

All I Know of Astronomy

When you swim my thighs with your fingers,
We look like two galaxies touching.
Black body over black body.

And in my bed we're a Binary Star.
Orbiting so close to each other,
Your light and mine are convincingly one.

-

Love's a funny thing;
You have to keep risking and hoping
And hoping and risking

If you ever want any.

Some Wars Are Fought Under the Skin

I am the grand saboteur.
I am the creature that fights joy,
The thing that struggles to loosen itself from lonely.

I've got fear the size of a house.
And pain that likes to pester.
I am holding grudges in both hands.

Darling, my anxiety is brutal
And my doubts are persistent.

But your staying has always been true
And your love is tender.
And I'll fight myself to keep you.

After Everything

Honest to God,
I don't think I have enough teeth or tongue or mouth
To carry your name in conversation.

What was between us, cut clean and cruel.
And fell graceless.

Love that grows from a wound
Needs more tenderness than we gave it.

Because when it shakes the house,
Nothing survives.
Not a friendship, not a sweetness, not a mouth to
carry a name.

a fire like you

-

We end things how they started.
Over Frank Ocean and sex.
Kind water.

We end things without bruise.
Love, this time, was far from a danger.
It was just unsettled and thin.
But it died laughing.

-

Only a thing as kind as love
Can touch you
And make every bit of you feel blessed.

Your Joy Makes Up for Your Two Left Feet

I watch you dance in the home we've made
despite or because, with or without
I can't help but smile at the thought of all that
joy in one body
A body I am blessed to know rests beside mine
every night.

-

This once, you mean to stay. After all, this lover is warm, and as much as you've tried, you cannot find your father in his mouth. This once, you mean to love him back.

a fire like you

\-

The wisest beast within me says "Leave," and I obey.

Oh Sthandwa

Your love dances,
Is a radiant thing,
Warms any space,
Is loud and intentional,
And uncommonly kind.

Your love gets to the very soul of it.

Swoon

You came, and the poems gathered
and the walls fell
and my love was let loose

It Was Best Before

When love comes undone,
it isn't always life being brutal.

Some things are good until they are not.

-

I want to take you out of the city
To the vastness
To less smother
To watch the sky with new eyes
And see life as it was meant.

a fire like you

-

I have decided to never again put myself through
hell for love.
This life is far too delicious to be spent burning
for men.

-

You like to gather at my thighs
And want me,
Want me badly but not entirely.

You promise things you're not set on giving.
You lie and moan through the teeth.

a fire like you

"Endure" Is a Filthy Word

Love doesn't mean to make light out of all the
darkness, meal out of bone, enough out of too little.

Milk

I have seen so many loves thrown out.
I am sorry that I keep asking if you'll stay.
I can't seem to shake the fear that we'll sour each other.

Where All Loves Ought to Start

I am sorry in a thousand languages for ever giving myself up for you.

I fooled us both.

I was the lover I needed most.

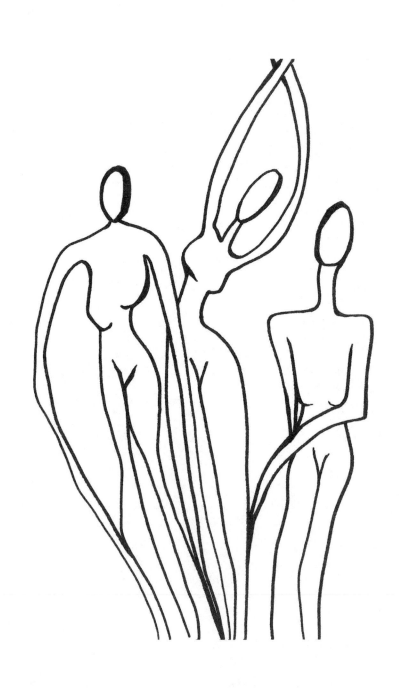

Sister

Nectar

One day our mothers may ask
"Who do you love completely?"
May we grow to respond
"Ourselves. Ourselves. Our lovely selves."

Anaiah's Poem

I was in the room when you first graced the world
with your breath,
Yelling and crying,
We heard you then, and we have heard you now.
Make us hear you always.

Learning to Friendship

I am learning to be more thoughtful in my healing.
Please stop me if all I put on your plate is in my pain.
Real love is a full meal,
And friends don't let friends starve.

Deliverance

If you find yourself very black and very tired,
Very tired and very black,
Very woman and very black and very tired,

Rest and mean it.

Ambushing Goodness

You are stubborn in your sorrow. Adamant on being
unkind to yourself.
I could shake you for it.

When I've found you again dancing in the drink,
acting joy, poorly,
I want to pull you out from under it all.

Clean you.

Give you what love I can.

Wait with you on the corner for good things to come.

The Loveliest of Loves

You always calm the broken things in me.
You lift me above myself.
You are a sister and a home.
You are a kingdom of forgiving.
I am sorry if you've ever had to stretch your life
for me.

All bonds bend, but if this life has given me anything,
it's the blessing of being loved by you.

a fire like you

-

Sis wam,

Share some of your peace.
Teach me how to wrap myself around myself
And be certain in it.

May This Poem Meet You In Your Language

Mothers who crossed oceans for their children's joy
To live in forms
And lines
And checks

In hand-me-downs and stare-me-downs

In a language you may never sit in comfortably.
A language with no back to carry your meaning.

In missing home
While making your children a new one.

You deserve adoration.
Your stories are the ones we are waiting for.

Let Black Girls Be

I was born on a Wednesday.
Raised a good black child with bubbles in her hair.
Quiet and curious, at first,
quieter and less curious, later.
Where does it go, this fearlessness and hunger for
the world?
Who kills it in black girls?

To be a black girl is a thing of grace.
If I am ever a mother to one,
I hope she never falls into doubt with herself.
I hope she doesn't hesitate
to eat the room and everyone in it.
I hope she is loud and certain of herself.

Existing can be done in the quiet,
but black girls,
black girls weren't meant for that kind of thing.
Black girls were made for boldness and
boundlessness.

a fire like you

-

When you are ready,
come up for air,
beloved,
we are waiting for you with tenderness.

Window

In my mother's living room, I sit in my grief.

And she stirs so much, you'd think she was dancing.

She's not used to seeing the insides out.
In me, she is seeing a sadness she keeps quiet in herself.

Imagine that,
never having the privilege to listen to your pain?

Imagine that,
never knowing you had the right to fall apart?

How many women's stories go untold?
How many parts of our mothers have never seen the light?

a fire like you

-

Mum,

When you tell me your story, you don't have to cut
off the crusts.
You can't mother your way out of the truth.

Each of You

Sis wam,
Home is going mad.
Home is a wound.
We are always looking for you.

Sis wam,
We are missing in our own lives.
Our lives are filled with missing you.

Sis wam,
We are lost too.

*Every day, more missing girls. Every day, stories
cut short.

This Too Is a Love Poem

Mama,

I know you never meant to teach me fear
or how to look danger in the eye and crave it,
but here we are.

Here we are,
alive and willing,
and that's all you need to be to learn something new.

a fire like you

-

You owe yourself a warm life,
peopled with only those who feed that fire.

Now You Know

All along,
since the beginning of the beginning,
you've been worthy.

So,
you've got to start giving a damn about yourself.

Sister

Come and bask in this joy with me;
I am here because you held my hand.

Your sisterhood has made this terror of a life
light and breathable.

A Note on the Illustrations

Thank you dearly to Lulama Wolf (@lulamawolf) and Neo Phage (@n_phage) for the beautiful illustrations. It is an honor to bring my work to life with the support and guidance of other African women artists.

Acknowledgments

To my literary agents at Folio Literary Management, Katherine Latshaw and Erin Harris, I am deeply indebted. Thank you for believing in me.

To my editor Melissa Zahorsky, Kirsty Melville, Kathy Hilliard, and everyone at Andrews McMeel, thank you for giving my words and me a home.

Mum, Dad, Sarai, Akuzike, Ngawina, and Gome, Anthony, Micah, Jeremy, Luca, Jaxon, Ezekiel, and Anaiah, I am blessed to have you.

To all my dearest friends, you are the warm ones, and I cannot thank you enough for always showing me grace. Liliana, Katy, Ines, Sharon, Bongeka, Iyone, Tchie, Bilphena, and all the other stars of my life.

Thank you to everyone who has ever made me feel like my work is necessary.

And finally, to Sakhe, I don't have the range or the words or even the language. You are everything.

Enjoy *a fire like you* as an audiobook narrated by the author, wherever audiobooks are sold.

UPILE CHISALA is a storyteller from Malawi and a graduate of the University of Oxford. Known for her short and powerful poems, she is the author of the books *soft magic* and *nectar. a fire like you* is her third collection of poetry and prose. She lives in Johannesburg, South Africa.

Andrews McMeel Publishing
a division of Andrews McMeel Universal
1130 Walnut Street, Kansas City, Missouri 64106

www.andrewsmcmeel.com

20 21 22 23 24 BVG 10 9 8 7 6 5 4 3 2 1

ISBN: 978-1-4494-9958-7

Library of Congress Control Number: 2019954348

Editor: Melissa Zahorsky
Art Director/Designer: Julie Barnes
Production Editor: Elizabeth A. Garcia
Production Manager: Cliff Koehler

ATTENTION: SCHOOLS AND BUSINESSES
Andrews McMeel books are available at quantity discounts with
bulk purchase for educational, business, or sales promotional use.
For information, please e-mail the Andrews McMeel Publishing
Special Sales Department: specialsales@amuniversal.com.